Metal Detector Detective

by Linda Lott
illustrated by Nicole Wong

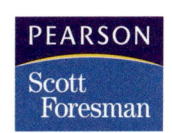

PEARSON
Scott Foresman

Editorial Offices: Glenview, Illinois • Parsippany, New Jersey • New York, New York
Sales Offices: Needham, Massachusetts • Duluth, Georgia • Glenview, Illinois
Coppell, Texas • Ontario, California • Mesa, Arizona

Every effort has been made to secure permission and provide appropriate credit for photographic material. The publisher deeply regrets any omission and pledges to correct errors called to its attention in subsequent editions.

Unless otherwise acknowledged, all photographs are the property of Scott Foresman, a division of Pearson Education.

Photo locators denoted as follows: Top (T), Center (C), Bottom (B), Left (L), Right (R), Background (Bkgd)

Illustrations by Nicole Wong

Photograph 12 Omni-Photo Communications, Inc.

ISBN: 0-328-13343-4

Copyright © Pearson Education, Inc.

All Rights Reserved. Printed in the United States of America. This publication is protected by Copyright, and permission should be obtained from the publisher prior to any prohibited reproduction, storage in a retrieval system, or transmission in any form by any means, electronic, mechanical, photocopying, recording, or likewise. For information regarding permission(s), write to: Permissions Department, Scott Foresman, 1900 East Lake Avenue, Glenview, Illinois 60025.

7 8 9 10 V0G1 14 13 12 11 10 09 08

Joe had been bored earlier that day. Luckily, his grandmother had invited him over to visit. Now Joe was sitting with her on her porch and drinking lemonade.

Grandma's neighbor, Ms. Choi, was visiting too. Suddenly Joe saw something on the porch that he hadn't seen before.

"What's that?" Joe asked.

"That's my metal detector," Grandma answered. "Here, I'll show you and Ms. Choi how to use it."

Joe and Ms. Choi watched as Grandma turned on the machine. "It's fun," she said. "When it beeps, I know a metal object is hiding below. Then I search until I find it."

"Wow!" said Joe. "May I try it later?"
Knowing that Joe liked to collect coins, Grandma said, "Of course you may! You might find a few coins for your collection!"

They all sat down on Grandma's porch again. "Whew!" Ms. Choi said. "I love my big garden, but caring for it is a lot of work." She reached for her lemonade but stopped suddenly. She looked upset.

There was a strain in her voice as she spoke. "I've lost my special ring," she cried. "It belonged to my grandmother. It must have fallen into my garden!"

"Don't worry, Ms. Choi," Joe said. "I'll find your ring for you!"

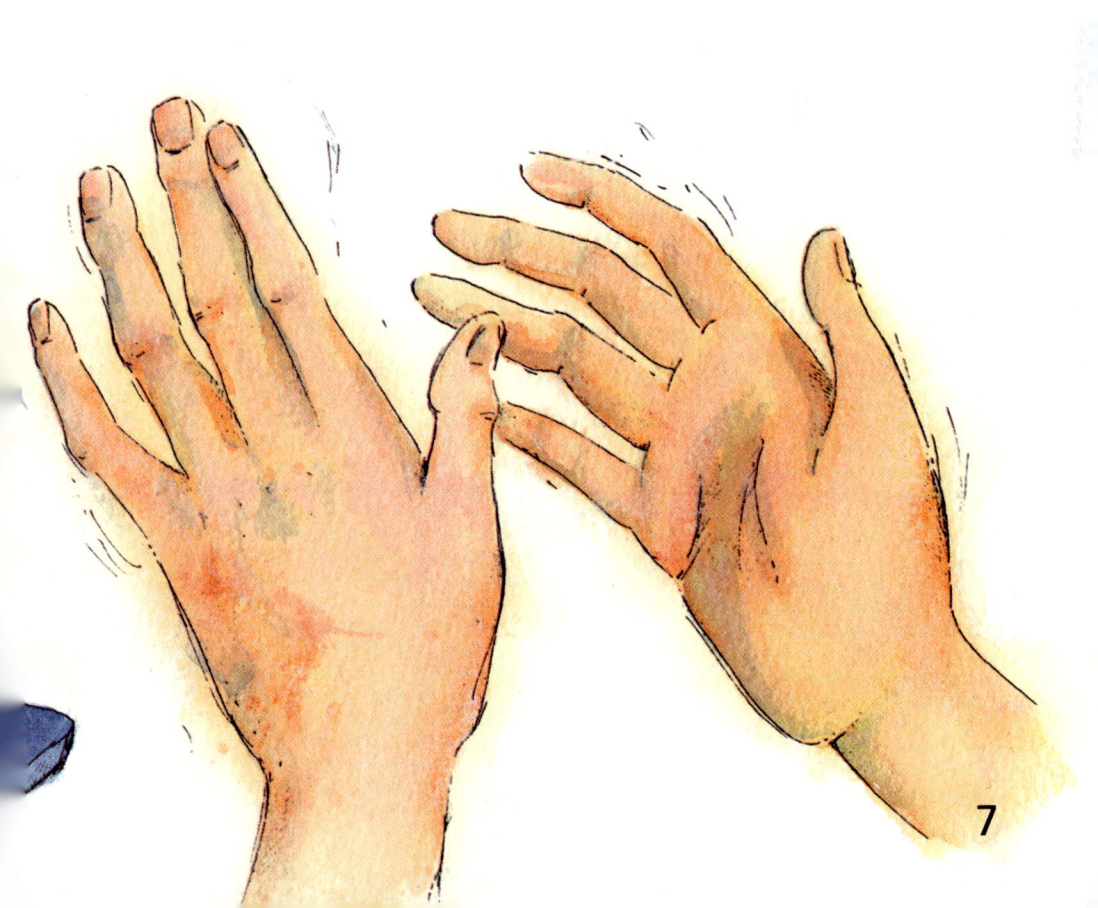

Joe quickly realized that he had taken on an enormous task. Ms. Choi's whole yard was a garden! Joe needed more information to narrow his search. "Where were you working?" he asked.

"Everywhere!" explained Ms. Choi. "The ring will be too hard to find, Joe!"

Then Joe and Grandma had an idea. Joe ran for the metal detector.

He searched the flowerbeds. When the machine beeped, he dug up bent nails.

Next, Joe looked in the bushes. The machine beeped again. This time, Joe happily picked up some scattered coins.

Joe kept trying. The machine beeped a third time. Joe gently parted the ivy that covered the ground. Suddenly he spotted something shiny. It was a gold ring!

Joe ran over and handed the ring to Ms. Choi. "Oh, thank you!" she said. "I'm going to give you a reward, Joe!"

"You've already given me my reward," Joe said. "You helped me decide how to keep myself busy this summer. I'm going to be a metal detector detective!"

Before You Go Out Searching

Using a metal detector can be a fun hobby. Before you go out metal detecting, though, there are some rules you must learn to follow.

Metal detectors are not allowed on National Park Service lands. Those places include national sea coasts, federal parks, historic battlefields and markers, and Native American burial grounds. Also, there are many other places, such as public schools, churches, and private lands, where you must ask permission before you use a metal detector.

If you're ever in doubt about whether you can use a metal detector, just ask! You can also go onto the Internet and look for information about groups that use metal detectors. Happy searching!

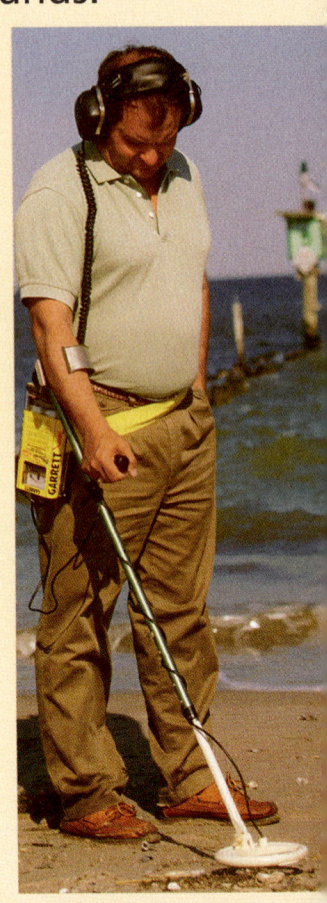